THE

DIGITAL

PULPIT

NOLAN W. McCANTS

The Digital Pulpit
Pivoting from Physical to Virtual Church

Nolan W. McCants

© 2021 Nolan W. McCants

Printed in the United States of America

ISBN: 978-0-9894935-3-6

CONTENTS

"

In times of change learners
inherit the earth; while the
learned find themselves
beautifully equipped to
deal with a world that no
longer exists.

– Eric Hoffer

INTRODUCTION

There has been a seismic shift produced by the COVID-19 global pandemic, and church leaders everywhere are scrambling, trying to figure out what to do next in response to this unexplained and unanticipated phenomenon. As though we were being prepared, disruption in recent years has become a norm, as social media, globalization and technology has changed the game in just about every area of life.

Over the last several years, around the world it is clear that something had shifted. Church attendance in many places is declining. Financial resources are drying up as contributions have dropped. Regular church goers are growing weary of many practices that had been a part of the worship experience for many generations. Today, Boomers, Gen Xers and Millennials alike, have become intolerable of most anything previously held sacred, thus earning the title "The Cancel Generation." Traditions that have been passed down and accepted without scrutiny by older generations are being rejected without apology.

During a meeting in Douala, Cameroon, in August 2019, I spoke about this season of disruption, emphasizing the fact that we need to embrace this new reality. "It's all about change," I explained, change that was pushing the church outside of the walls and challenging some norms. I have long sensed that God was moving us into a new era and this new reality was a part of it.

I had stated that we needed to embrace this change and consider new and radical ways of doing ministry. I especially encouraged the young Millennials to continue exploring ways of reaching their generation. There was a clear divide in the room, as the younger attendees applauded my call to loosen up, while the older generation seemed perplexed that I would encourage what was interpreted as defiance with its accompanying attitudes and behaviors. These behaviors were essentially viewed as rebellion and a rejection of the gospel—at least and perhaps a rejection of the gospel.

With Covid-19 affecting every sphere of life, many churches have scrambled to make adjustments in an attempt to meet this unprecedented challenge. Others have dug in deep with a resolve to hold to the way things have always been. Many see these attitudes and actions as an affront to God and His church, so with any adjustments to accommodate any change amounts to compromising the gospel.

Uncertainty has lingered in the air as church practices as we have known them are fading fast. Some even fear that America will become like much of Europe, a spiritually bankrupt nation, where grand cathedrals have been emptied or closed. Many of those beautiful monuments with their stained-glass windows and towering steeples have since been sold and turned into mosques, night clubs and retail outlets. With all of these dramatic, changes no one could have fathomed the impact of what was right around the corner.

COVID-19, a global pandemic that has turned everything on its head, is an epic disruption without discrimination. Governments, business, education, media, global travel, healthcare, the church and more have all been shaken. Fear, panic and despair have gripped the entire world, as this invisible and very aggressive deadly disease has moved rapidly, taking lives and sparing none—the rich, poor, young and old.

For the Church this has meant forced immersion. Much in the same way persecution drove the Church out of the comforts of Jerusalem, the Pandemic has forced us out of our business-as-usual complacency. With doors closed, people scattered and all norms shattered, the Church has been challenged to find new, innovative ways to sustain community, communicate the gospel and minister to a troubled and hurting world.

All of the props are gone. No alluring buildings, no sacred pulpit spaces, no melodious choirs, no worship bands, no amens and no lobby coffee klatches. We are now disoriented, and our spiritual equilibrium is off. What do we do and how do we do it? What are the lessons?

All of the systems, strategies and programming that have been perfected are now rendered useless. Staff and volunteers that we have poured into to create a functional cohesive team are now displaced. Overnight, we have been forced to pivot and find new ways to do ministry. What has been an add-on to our bank of marketing options, has now become our primary way of ministry. We must now shift to the Digital Pulpit, utilizing a mix of texting, social media, live streaming, emailing and video conferencing to reach our audiences, new and old.

Early during the Pandemic, many leaders resisted the shift, holding out for things to return to normal. Some were and still are disoriented and frustrated, in search for normalcy. They have been found defiantly grasping for business as usual, often taking to social media to complain and war against the imminent change that had already breached the horizon. Some thought this would simply be a short-term inconvenience. But, with our government failing to get ahead of the Pandemic, sweeping quarantines have left no options. Not to mention that people no longer felt comfortable gathering *en masse,* even if it is permitted. The fear of this disease has gripped the hearts of people everywhere.

In my 24 years of pastoring, we have only closed our doors once on a Sunday due to weather. We have, however, always stayed up on technology, incorporating various tech tools to enhance what we do as a ministry, to increase productivity or to manage various business functions. For example, our website contains information about ministry activities, our email list is up to date for members and guests, we have instituted online giving, offering a level of comfort with continuing giving this way. For years, we have experimented with streaming and the use of video technology. In fact, we have provided assistance to ministries around the world to help them in some of these areas, and we have also created a solid network of resources. Sadly, many churches have failed to stay current, and as a consequence, transition into this new era has been incredibly difficult. Many are still struggling to make changes.

We must acquaint ourselves with growing comfortable with adaptation, agility and fluidity, as these will need to become a part of our new normal. One thing is clear: We will either bend with these transitions to survive, or remain rigid and break. My goal is to have a testimony of effective change that leads to the effective making of powerful disciples from behind *The Digital Pulpit*.

What does all of this mean for ministers and ministries? How has this new era redefined ministry and what might the future bring?

The Digital Pulpit is an examination of this dramatic shift and I will offer some suggestions about how we might navigate this dynamic change. We will look at what might be temporary and what might remain; what might God be saying to the church and what might be a proper response.

I am convinced that we are in the midst of a great awakening and much needed reformation. I hope this writing proves to be fruitful in giving you perspective, encouragement and inspiration as you embrace the future of ministry in a post-pandemic era.

"Life imposes things on you that you can't control, but you still have the choice of how you're going to live through this."

– Celine Dion

NO TIME
TO THINK

Gloria and I had just returned from a ministry trip to Ghana, West Africa, up north in Tamale. We left at the onset of the Pandemic, and although things had heated up in the United States, we hadn't received any information so we kept our commitment. I was a little concerned about passing through Europe with all of the security checks and such, but decided to press on. I had traveled to Africa so many times, including during the Ebola outbreak, so I knew the drill. Leaving America was uneventful. Passing through Europe, the same. When we arrived in Ghana, they were fully equipped with thermometers and thermal imaging fever detection equipment. They were ready. Thankfully. we were able to pass through all checks and enter the country without any challenges.

On the return, screeners were a bit more aggressive and I had a scary moment. I had caught a cold and had a few COVID symptoms, including sneezing, coughing and a terrible runny nose. But thankfully no fever. I was able to clear security and all screening check points without any issues. Once on the flight, a gentleman spoke to a flight attendant and mentioned experiencing some discomfort. He was immediately escorted off the plane. I couldn't wait for the plane to take off as I was disinterested in being next to disembark.

Passing through Europe, there was still little-to-no COVID screening. Arriving at O'Hare International Airport here in Chicago, we were amazed to see absolutely no screening. It was a great trip as there was good receptivity to the teaching and we could sense an easy flow of the Spirit.

The Pandemic was just hitting Europe and China, and they were on full lockdown. It had not hit America nor Africa too hard at this point. Information was still sketchy, especially in the US. Once home, borders began closing, travel restrictions were issued and news of outbreaks began to spread.

That Sunday, I decided to have a brief, no hugs, distancing service. I suggested that the aged and anyone with underlining health issues should feel free to remain at home. There was a little tension and apprehension in the air that day; we had not received any concrete instructions from the government and no one really knew exactly how this virus was being transmitted. The service went off well. It was comforting to see everyone, especially having been abroad. Attendance was down about 30 percent. I gave instruction at the close of service that everyone should quickly say their goodbyes, not linger and move to their cars immediately afterwards. I closed the service, retreated to my office and then exited out of the back door. I knew I had a responsibility to lead through this coming crisis and keep everyone safe. In my mind, I had already prepared for not returning to the building until we had a clear sense of where things were headed.

After this service, there was no time to think. The Pandemic rolled across the US so fast and none of us had ever experienced anything like this. All we could do was react to things as they emerged, as was the case with every other church. We acted in the moment, having no advance warning, preparation or plans in place. Hoping to do the right things, God clearly provided the strength, wisdom and grace to navigate this delicate situation.

The Pivot

We now had a week to scramble and pivot, and to find a way to gather outside of our physical space. We had never encountered such upheaval. The one tool that we had used as a congregation, one that everybody was familiar and comfortable with, was a free teleconferencing service. We had used it for many years prior for meetings, book reads and other small gatherings. But never the entire church. It had been in place as an added convenience, when meeting in person was impractical for whatever reason. So, we took to the phones. We scheduled our time to match the regularly 10:00 am Sunday worship service. We sent emails and texts to our membership, alerting them about the teleconference. We called it Virtual Fellowship Sunday. Unfortunately, this was our first mistake, as every other church apparently had the same idea to use free teleconferencing at the same time. It was an absolute disaster and it remained so for several weeks following. We had jammed lines and people were getting busy signals or dropped calls. All sorts of noises could be heard during service, as not everyone was proficient at muting and unmuting. The chime rang every time someone entered the call and every time the frustrated left. It was an experience I would certainly leave off of my resume.

Some of our leaders were warning me that we would lose the people, due to their frustration. I don't think they realized the level of exasperation I was experiencing. It was truly a moment that tested my patience and my leadership. Could I pull us through this without adding to the panic that was already mounting? I was determined to remain calm, refusing to be overwhelmed and appear flustered.

I informally brought a small group together to begin searching for viable options. I needed those who could roll with me without being emotional or leaning into the wrong priorities. My concentration was on ease of use, capacity and reliability. My wife Gloria was extremely helpful in vetting the available services. She has a keen technical mind and can move quickly to figure things out. We worked together to think everything through that was put before us. There were others on the team to whom I handed assignments to get us on course.

I had no fear of loss. I was thinking as a father and telling everyone, "We have to keep the family together through this. We need everyone to feel a sense of connection, support and grounding in the things of God." They needed to see our faith work in real time in the midst of a global pandemic.

We opted for a more intimate virtual gathering space that would allow us to feel a sense of community. We ultimately decided to go with Webex, a video conferencing platform, much like Zoom, that we felt was more robust.

It took some time to figure out the platform. But, once we did, we were quickly able to ramp up, recapture our fading audience and develop various creative gathering opportunities that reconstructed the sense of community we had always enjoyed. We also decided to launch a content-rich digital newsletter each week that was chocked full of useful and current information about the Pandemic, family photos, music playlists, updates on ministry activities and articles written by current and past members. I felt this would up the engagement and broaden the ministry footprint. It was an overwhelming success and valued ministry tool. Our open rate for this weekly publication was incredibly high. So, we started to share our ideas with our entire mailing list and soon other ministries were borrowing from the concept, which we loved. (Part of our mission is to be a support to the global body of Christ.) We also started to see guests show up during our gatherings. Before long, we recognized that our attendance had become stronger virtually than when we were in our physical space. Something beautiful and unexpected was emerging from this daunting ordeal.

God was clearly trying to show us something, and like many I can feel a shift. Not everyone is open to the idea. But it is my opinion that we will never return to church as usual, and this change is for the good. While there was no time to think at the onset, we have since had time to think a lot—think about the past, the present and all of the possibilities of an exciting future. I say, if you are a senior leader, invite your leadership, staff and congregation to reimagine ministry. There are new practices to be adopted and some old to let die. Be courageous people of faith, depending on the Holy Spirit to guide you into this new era. Let's meet the challenge of a new day by faith and in faith.

"Learning how to respond to and master the process of change—and even to excel at it—is a critical leadership skill for the twenty-first century. Constant, rapid change will be a fact of life for all of us."

– Jennifer James

THE DIGITAL PULPIT

On a particular Sunday, instead of standing confidently behind my all-too-familiar fixed pulpit, wearing my Sunday best, with lights glaring and microphone in hand, I was dressed casually and seated comfortably at my kitchen table. It was a brand-new day!

While I started in the kitchen, then moved to the dining room and at times in other areas of my home, eventually I was mandated to the library. There were one too many, "Quiet I'm going virtual." commands, along with a mess of myriad of scattered electronics strewn all over the place. It reminded me of the way we started our fledgling church plant; the church it seemed at times was all over the house. I eventually took the time to arrange everything I needed to make the home library a comfortable and functional working studio from which I would engage my varied audiences.

However, on that Sunday while in the kitchen, I thought, *How ironic*. In every home the kitchen tends to be the default gathering place. It's where stories are told, traditions passed down, memories shared and lessons are taught. It's an intimate space where defenses are down. It's where laughter can be heard. This seemly sacred family space was the initial place to connect virtually with my church, friends and family. Until necessity mandated that I move from the kitchen, I had made some new friends and attracted regulars from across the country. Furnished with my laptop computer, now-standard ring light, Blue Yeti microphone and cell phone, this had become my digital pulpit, the place from where I navigated virtual ministry activities, sharing Kingdom principles, values and eternal truths. In fact, at some point, most rooms in my house had become my digital pulpit. Simply amazing!

I've held virtual board meetings, met with pastors, conducted business, hosted prayer meetings and Sunday fellowships, moderated global conversations on Facebook Live and gathered entrepreneurs to inspire and encourage. In reality, the Pandemic has proven to provide a world of new possibilities and opportunities. My pulpit is no longer fixed, impersonal or predictable. It has become fluid, intimate and without boundaries. We now have face-to-face visuals in a highly visual world. People can relate, seeing that we live just like they live. I see all of this as being in the Spirit of Jesus joining folks in their homes. It's like the first century church, moving virtually from house to house—simple, powerful and yet still highly effective.

Being in my home and not having the time to consider all of the resulting consequences, one exciting discovery has been the experience of a welcomed invasion of my privacy. People whom I'd loved and some I was meeting for the first time have had the opportunity to peek inside of my personal space. And, for those who elected to turn on their cameras, me into theirs. Some connect from their homes, some from their patios, others in their cars or even at work. I get glimpse into their lives through meaningful moments. It has introduced an entirely new, unexpected, up close and positive personal relationship dynamic.

A New Preaching Dynamic

Preaching from my digital pulpit was awkward at first. No longer standing, I'm now seated. I can see the people, but I can't hear them; they're all muted. They can all see and hear me, but are not able to respond verbally with a joyous, "Amen!" or celebratory, "Praise God!" Some have their cameras turned on and others opt to have theirs off, just listening. With no audible responses, we suggested making a hand clapping gesture in their cameras to signal an amen—anything to encourage the speaker.

My digital pulpit has removed the theatrics and fillers. No musical interludes or pauses for the applauses and amens, just a straight-forward, clean delivery of good sound teaching ... as I suppose it should be.

A digital pulpit meant an immediate stretching and adjusting to this dramatic change. It was no longer the way I had grown accustomed to over the past few decades. Like with any new challenge, the thoughts arose: Can I pull this off successfully? Will the people go for this new method? Nevertheless, I pressed into it, making corrections as I went. You see, I'm that guy who's not afraid of new, different, innovative or even the strange (I've been called that a time or two). So, my attitude was, *Let's do this and see where it leads.*

Over the past weeks, I've really been thinking that the way things are going is no mistake. I can sense the creative genius of the Holy Spirit at work in it all and I want to be a part of His work.

Nine months in

In what I call the "new Church era," there is a new buzz term: virtual ministry. However, it hasn't taken long for this to become a well-worn term. It's now known that ministry can happen anywhere, reaching an unlimited audience. It's just a matter of attracting people to your platform. The Church online is not a new concept or means of doing ministry, however, the global pandemic has meant a far greater dependence upon the virtual world, and for those who have fought this movement, baptism by fire has been their lot. Options are few and many have been thrust into the us technology who have been resistant to th It's a new day. The church has left the The game has changed and the pla been leveled. Mega churches, sto those in the city and those in the country, those in America and abroad—all have been impacted and forced to shift.

It's been several months since we left our building and taken everything online. To my amazement we've held steady numbers in attendance and financial support *and* we've actually broadened our reach and support.

We have created three primary "connection points," a phrase we've adopted during the Pandemic to describe the various ways to access the ministry. Ala carte style, you pick the connection points that work for you and jump in. No shaming, no guilting, these are all open spaces available for people to connect and be fed without feeling the need to join anything.

Boundless Sunday is now our standard worship ser- 0 minutes. It seems ess is best. *VGroups* sort of a small group /e also offer a week- cellent way to start all of the stress and ing, we meet each passage and offer

e of
e idea.
building.
ying field has
refront churches,

prayer around our findings. We call it *DayStart* and it's very popular.

This foundation of our virtual ministry has proven to be very insightful and liberating. Insightful in that there seems to be a different level of commitment for those who show up in these virtual spaces; liberating because the pressure to fill a physical space is removed. The virtual space essentially expands and contracts real time in a truly organic way. This is our attempt to be responsive, courageous and adaptive.

**"The only way to predict
the future is to shape the
future."**

– Eric Hoffer

EMERGING
MODELS

In life, change is a given. And our world is undergoing unprecedented change—including the Church world! It's happened and continues to happen. There's no denying and definitely no controlling it. We must respond and it's time to focus less on limitations and restrictions and more on possibilities, for both now and the future. Meanwhile, there are many leaders who are unwilling to accept this reality. They simply want to return to the status quo, wanting nothing to do with the thought of virtual ministry, particularly as a possible replacement of physical gatherings on any level. They prefer seeing this crisis as a temporary condition and unwanted disruption that will soon end. The thought of no longer coming together in a building is quite disturbing to them. Fear, apprehension and concern for the future has gripped the hearts of some leaders, who have become paralyzed by fear and are consequently unable to move forward.

The common questions heard among leaders are; Where is all of this going? Will the Church survive this extended period of isolation? Or will some people just stop attending local churches altogether? This one thing is true: we can't afford to be shortsighted or fearful. We must adapt and consider new models. We've got to tap into the creative mind of God. Again, I stress that we are in a moment of time in which untold possibilities are before us. However, if we would fear not and continue to forge ahead, I am certain that God will help us successfully navigate these turbulent times.

We have already begun to see a variety new ministry models emerging—some strategic, very deliberate and well thought out. Others are just a reaction with the thought to survive in what has proven to be trying times for many. What I've gathered in talking to leaders from around the world is there is no one-size-fits-all model. There are many factors that dictate the methods in which ministry is carried out during this Pandemic. These factors are shaping thoughts about what a post-pandemic Church might look like.

For the post-pandemic Church, we must now consider things such as a congregation's level of familiarity with technology, their access to stable WIFI and whether such technology is even afford-able. The way people have been socialized can also be a factor. One church leader in the Republic of Benin noted that the Beninese are very private, so in-home ministry as an option was improbable. A pastor in Cameron, on the other hand, found the current Covid crisis to be an ideal opportunity to grow home ministries. Her church's answer to the dilemma of limited WIFI access was to identify those in the congregation with access and technol-ogy, then have these people host smaller. more in-timate meetings in their area. Services would then be streamed from their church into the homes. Parishioners could then gather together for prayer and comforting one another.

Here in America, I've seen pastors preaching in full clergy garb, standing behind a podium in their living rooms, some in transformed garages and others outdoors in open spaces. Many are using a hybrid strategy, combining social media with video conferencing or other technological meth-ods. Other pastors have taken to the pulpits in their churches where they produced full services, flawlessly packaged and professionally executed to serve up to their audiences. Depending on the locale, some have already returned to their buildings with scaled back attendance, while others have turned to live streaming on social media or on their church website. At this point, we're all in varied stages of experimentation and discovery, and in search of the right mix. All are seeking to find what works in their context to keep ministry alive and progressing.

There have also been some unexpected benefits that have surfaced as well. In many cases, pastors have been forced by necessity to entrust some of their pastoral care responsibilities to lay people. The result has been the emergence of new leaders stepping into roles normally held exclusively by "trained professionals." We have been pressed into rediscovering some biblical models where believers are actually equipped to do the work of ministry. If we are intentional, we will see more of this returning to biblical norms. This could play well into the church returning to health.

I am encouraging all in my circle to stay loose and not commit to anything as being permanent. I think it's also important to communicate this message to the congregation as well. Things will continue to evolve and morph, and we will need to continue to adapt and adjust. Just as the world is being reshaped, so will ministry. I want to encourage you to see this critical time in history as a God moment of opportunity, rather than an insurmountable problem.

Digital Tools

There are a variety of digital tools available to fuel your digital pulpit. Below is my short list. By employing the right mix and a fluid way to use these, they can be executed in a harmonious, complimentary way to deliver comprehensive, quality ministry. In planning, it is essential that you have a clear, realistic set of objectives in place. Knowing what you're trying to achieve will dictate which tools to use and when.

Thriving in this new era will mean leaders must be clear on priorities and act on them. Is it filling seats or filling hearts? Being cute or being effective? Making fans or making disciples? You have to determine what you are looking to achieve. The swiftness of change and the revealing of hearts, minds and well-worn, dated practices has placed a demand on leaders, and selecting the right tools and mix will speak to this.

This list is not by any means comprehensive and is sure to grow as technology expands to accommodate this new virtual world. These are some of the more familiar tools being used thus far:

Digital Tool Mix Short List

- Social Media *(Facebook, Instagram, YouTube)*
- Streaming broadcast of Live services
- Website
- Teleconferencing
- Videoconferencing (Zoom, Webex, Microsoft Teams)
- Email
- Text
- WhatsApp
- Videos

The use of digital tools will also mean taking a closer look at how we staff our ministries going forward. We will need more tech savvy people who are up to speed on existing technology and have an eye on current trends. We are already hearing various staff titles like Pastor of Technology and Social Media Minister. There's a need to become more proficient in the use of such tools and become more aggressive in integrating them into our strategies.

Collaboration

Collaboration will be one of our best and most timely strategies. This is a great time to consider coming together to solve our collective problems, as no one has gone unscathed during the Pandemic. In my case, I have found it very helpful and comforting to engage in dialogue with leaders from different places to talk about how they are working through everything. I am seeking to learn from them and hopefully to share something that will encourage, embolden and add to their explorations. I see this as godly interaction that can bring us back to the place where we see ourselves as one body seeking to bring glory to God, and not as competitors acting as though we're called to build our own small kingdoms. Whether in a formally arranged gathering or periodic, informally connecting to exchange ideas and give progress reports, we can all learn from one another. Small church leaders have perspective and larger church leaders have perspective. Those in varied locations view things differently. It all matters. In collaborating, we will see to it that the Church enriches itself in love, while sharing the resources of creativity, knowledge and innovation.

"

"Vulnerability is the birthplace of innovation, creativity and change."

– Brene Brown

OUT OF THE BOX

No one could have predicted a world event that would force churches to leave their buildings and find alternate ways of delivering ministry. But it has happened and it was frightening, particularly having had nothing in recent history to compare to that could have prepared any of us for this.

Trusting that God is in control and will guide us through every experience is now a big deal. While this global crisis has a down side, not everything has been unfavorable. The overwhelming angst experienced by church leaders and church goers alike at the onset of the Pandemic has been countered by some unexpected benefits and blessings. It's not uncommon for such a thing to occur; we serve a good God who remains faithful and mindful of all that we experience. He has a proven track record of stepping into the midst of the worst of events and manifesting boundless blessings. Being pushed out of the church-as-always box has been no different.

We are nearly a year in, the dust has settled a bit and we have managed to resume ministry on some level, albeit differently. There have been discoveries and serendipitous revelations that have expanded our thoughts about how to do ministry—at least it's that way for those who are open to see and accept these new realities.

I am primarily addressing those things that have surfaced with the use of virtual ministry in this chapter. The response to out-of-the-box ministry has been far more fruitful than one would ever have expected. While informally surveying some leaders worldwide, here are some things that have contributed to their present fruitfulness. In addition to those listed, we must also be careful to credit the dynamic and creative work of the Holy Spirit to explain this movement.

This should not be viewed as an argument for or against virtual ministry as the only alternative to be employed. I still believe there is a need for gathering, although the way that looks may ultimately change. These are just some observations to ponder as we navigate this new frontier.

Accountability Shift

People have responded to ministry in virtual spaces in unexpected and wonderful ways. They are more present, attentive and actively engaged beyond what has occurred in our physical spaces. There appears to be an unforeseen accountability shift, where people have now begun assuming more personal responsibility for their own spiritual walk. We are seeing more intentionality, self-governance and self-initiating actions on the part of believers, as community engagement has increased. There could be many reasons for this, but here are a few considerations:

- Daily pressures brought on by the Pandemic.
- The realization that in isolation you must learn to fend for yourself.
- Perhaps there's a growing sense that when it comes to maintaining our health, safety and spirituality, there is a need for increased vigilance.

At the end of the day, these make for a healthier faith community. This shift in accountability will lead to individual spiritual growth and move us towards having mature believers who can then minister life to others. The greatest revelation is to ultimately see God as being the only constant in a world where everything can and has come unhinged overnight.

Convenience Factor

You can't deny the convenience factor for all involved: pastors, deacons, teachers, volunteers and attendees. Sunday morning is now a whole new thing. I'm already clear that not everyone is thrilled about this. "Going to church" has become such a static part of our culture. It's a long-held tradition that we believe to be very solidly backed by Scripture. In fact, for many it may be considered a sin to move to an online virtual fellowship versus a physical space. There is a doubt that this is a valid form of worship, and here are some observations made since the Pandemic that are very telling and show how people have responded to virtual services. It would be unwise to ignore these, as we forge ahead attempting to follow the lead of the Holy Spirit.

First of all, preparation is a whole lot easier, especially if there are children involved. You can enjoy breakfast, dress and be in front of your computer in a fraction of the time it takes to get everyone ready and moving towards the car. Oh man, the things swimming around in our heads: the car, the kids, what we forgot and how late we're going to be. There is also the weather factor, especially in the winter; not to mention, everyone is exhausted after a long work week, commutes, school and other family activities.

Many times, there are various responsibilities that family members may have once they've arrived at church. This can be further exacerbated when one family member has a responsibility that forces everyone in the house to leave early and just hang around until service gets started. Weekday Bible studies, small groups and ministry meetings are no longer a dreaded affair, after driving home from work. It used to be that people may squeeze in dinner with the family before rushing out of the door to church. (I'm exhausted from writing about this!) From behind the digital pulpit, what we are seeing is more on-time and consistent on-line attendance, as opposed to when in a building and everyone present is wearing a "broad" smile.

Time

It's funny, I can remember articles and various reports years ago that spoke of all the extra time we humans would enjoy, as computers would soon handle the mundane tasks and even some of the more complex ones for us. Ha! They missed big time on those projections. We are finding less and less time to do much of anything. It takes great discipline and determination to resist today's time snatchers. The Church has been in competition with a lot of these things over the past couple decades, and has not always won. More and more people were splitting their time between sports, family activities and various events that also required preparation and travel time. Then there are computers, tablets and mobile devices. Each week in shame, I look at the report that tells me how many hours I spent on my gadgets. People are very jealous of their time, yet many have no clue how to manage theirs. Saying NO seems to have become a lost art. The quality time that could have been spent in community with other believers is squandered. It would be interesting to see just how many hours a family saves by attending virtual services versus in-person physical services and events.

Less to Judge

One day, while thinking through all of the rapid changes, it occurred to me that with virtual ministry there is far less to judge. In physical spaces, there are countless passive distractions and we spend an awful lot of time judging them all. How many cars are there in the parking lot? Why aren't the safety cones out and in place? How is the room temperature? Is the crowd larger or smaller than last week? Who are the new people? I don't see the pastor. I'm not happy with where the ushers seated us today. The volunteers for the nursery are late again.

Honey, did you remember to bring the check book? You think the praise team was a little flat today? Who decorated for the meet-n-greet? Questions, distractions … so much to judge. With virtual ministry, attendees are comfortably situated in their own environment, where there is less to judge. All of the previously expended energy has now gone into listening, processing and responding to the truth that's being taught from behind the digital pulpit.

Anonymity

As our church has pretty much settled on video-conferencing for now, I'm sharing from this viewpoint. Just as in physical spaces, people aren't always comfortable with being engaged, particularly guests. We did fairly well with greeting visitors and making them feel welcomed. But it was still always a tricky balancing act, as we would have to sort of discern where their comfort levels were. In addition to visitors, we discovered that there were even members who didn't want, or perhaps need, the close social connection. They appeared more comfortable with coming and going while engaging on their terms.

The beauty of virtual ministry and particularly with the use of videoconferencing, I have noticed that guests and some of our more private members often feel more comfortable joining in without their cameras on. They can also elect not to show a name. It takes getting used to, but it seems to keep them coming and engaged. I like the idea of options, meeting people where they are, and journeying with them is Jesus-like.

Cost Savings

There is also the reality of cost savings. Many churches are finding a bump in contributions because parishioners are spending less on fuel, clothes and other preparations when attending physical services. It appears that many are using some of those savings to be more supportive of the ministry. At the same time, there are some savings to the church, as there are lowered costs in utilities, supplies and general upkeep costs.

Volunteerism

Finally, managing the recruitment and management of volunteerism can be daunting. Now that we're out of the box, the need for an army of volunteers has greatly diminished. Greeters, ushers, security and hospitality teams are no longer needed in a virtual scenario. All of these can be ultimately repurposed and possibly placed in positions to expand ministry offerings and outreach. New areas of ministry will continue to unfold, as we grow in understanding what the future church will look like.

"If you're not stubborn, you'll give up on experiments too soon. And if you're not flexible, you'll pound your head against the wall and you won't see a different solution to a problem you're trying to solve."

– Jeff Bezos

BEYOND THE STATUS QUO

It's amazing how quickly we forget the discomforts of a recent past, when new pain, strain and frustrations suddenly appear and eclipse the old. For several years now, many of us leaders have lamented the downturn in church attendance and the mounting disinterest in church as usual. Now COVID-19 has upstaged all of that and has given us something greater to be concerned about. Now the cry is, "When are we going to go back?" To which I ask, "Back to what?"

My personal confession is that I had really been growing more and more frustrated with the lackluster status quo as well. You know the "usual" tried-and-true way of doing church, with all of its mundane predictability. While we have always worked the edge and had done some creative out-of-the-box things as compared to others, I still felt we'd been held hostage to the restrictive ways of the past. There's something about familiarity, even when unhealthy, that people hold too. I suppose familiarity wears better than change. I guess it's true that old habits die hard.

The Church has a particular way of doing things that has been working for decades, if not centuries. No real thought is needed to employ it; it's pretty much like painting by numbers. All that was needed was a meeting space, a podium, some singing, preaching, a Bible study, maybe prayer, the exchange of niceties and then repeat. Oh, and a collection of offerings to help fund the work. Now, on the face of it, there is absolutely nothing improper about any of this. But the question that we may want to ask of ourselves is, "Was it really ministry or were we on autopilot?" Maybe even on life support, doing what we've always done, whether it produced the desired results or not. Had we lost focus on the main things and exchanged them for lifeless, religious activities that paid the bills? Had our focus turned towards maintaining those systems, no matter the cost?

Even the progressive ministries, with all of their creative innovations and use of multimedia and other technologies, have found themselves still locked into some of the traditional operational cycles. Mega churches and mega-like churches had managed to add menus of other features that sort of set them apart. But we soon discovered that highly curated programming was slowly replacing a dependence on the Holy Spirit, while branding, attendance and bottom lines had become more the focus. So, when you pulled back the skin, the same old bones could be found beneath them all. The bulk of time, energy and resources went into feeding and maintaining the machine.

Numeric growth only added to the challenge. Now, like a corporation, there were "shareholders" to appease if you will, people who had invested in the idea of a big "successful" ministry. But let's examine this so-called success for a moment. Less and less time, money and effort were spent on making disciples a part of the success equation. Were people really experiencing transformation? Most discussions surrounded the health and sustainability of the machine. So, the last thing anybody wanted to do was place a demand on attendees by challenging them to change, and taking the chance they wouldn't return. This is real talk ladies and gentlemen.

The Pandemic has interrupted all of this and forced us to think, and re-think, considering all of these realities. At the same time, there are many who still refuse to think, hoping this seismic shift is just an aberration. Head in the sand, they are laser focused on returning to the building to resume regularly scheduled programming.

Finally, please allow me to make some things clear before I continue. The point here is in no way an attempt to devalue and count as useless the practices of the past. Neither am I suggesting in any way that these were an ineffective waste. They worked well to serve numerous generations. However, it's clear that a shift in methodologies is needed to keep up with the times and we cannot afford to hold methods up as sacred. Periodic change is inevitable, needed and restorative. It may be that the Lord has helped us along, using the opportunity of a global pandemic to force us into some healthy transformative change.

Pioneers

Everyone is still reeling in shock over what has occurred in the world. We have found ourselves suspended in a space of uncertainty and adventure, where faith and confidence in God's guiding hand are essential. No one knows what the future Church will look like, but most will agree that it will no longer be the same. Since we are most comfortable with the familiar and cautious about the unknown, we will need to ask for God's help to let go of some things and embrace others, as we enter this new Church age. It's an exciting time of exploration!

The days of the cookie cutter, follow the leader, one-size-fits-all model are gone. We're being pressed into thinking outside of the proverbial box, now that the lid is off and the walls are down. During the Pandemic, people have tasted something refreshing, and there's no doubt they will demand more, and the digital pulpit is where they will turn.

There are new pioneers of necessity rising out of the day to aid our moving beyond the status quo. As we set out on this extraordinary journey, these new minds, voices and influencers will act courageously, with boldness and with a sensitivity to the voice of the Holy Spirit. A daunting challenge, these will have been gifted to see what's not been seen before, and then prompted to act on making those new visions a reality.

I further believe we will see a collaborative undertaking between the young, enthusiastic and imaginative, and the aged, experienced and sober minded. My prayer is that we would all have ears to hear and value the diversity of voices, and not just the popular.

As we begin to see the light of this new Church era, it can be expected that unconventional ideas, methods and strategies will arise. Prayerfully, we can embrace them and possess a shared willingness to explore, experiment and even fail while trying to implement them. I say it's an ideal time to let go of some past practices and give them a decent burial, allowing God to express Himself in new ways. May this new direction serve to accelerate the process of not just filling pews, but filling the whole earth with the knowledge of God. May we see a beautiful transformation of the nations and the manifestation of God's Kingdom on earth.

Lasting Change

We have seen the world shaken before, just not to this magnitude. In America, we saw 911 bring people out to church for prayer by the droves and then within months, as soon as the fear lifted, there was a return to the old ways. Is this time any different? Do we really see a need for real, wide-ranging change? Once we are able to freely come together in physical spaces without the fear of it being unsafe, will we just settle back into our old complacent ways?

Most people tend to think the world and the Church as we've known it will never be the same again. But only time will tell. I think it's critical to be mindful of the change and work needed to pursue *real* transformation, and not just the cheap route of whitewashing. This change has to be as much a spiritual one as one of function and methodologies. We need an awakening more than anything else!

If priority is still making disciples, who then is making disciples? Anything less may be celebrated by the world and comforting to our egos, but it falls short of being real Kingdom success.

These forced changes have caused me to pause and consider what the Holy Spirit might be up to in this epic moment in history. I want to be found flowing with the Spirit, not warring against it.

Some things we will keep and some things will need to be discarded. It's imperative that we look to the Lord to help us make those critical decisions. We will need to be led of the Spirit for lasting change—transformative top-to-bottom change. Our moving forward as the Church won't mean a dismantling as such, but more a reengineering to position us to bring glory to God.

May the wisdom of God guide us in this both now and in the future.

Biblical Discipleship

Just for clarity, I thought to define disciple and discipleship, as terms often lose their meaning or are redefined over time. Many have reduced the definition to mean an acceptance of Christ, conversion or entry into the Kingdom, often occurring at an evangelism event or during a service following an appeal. I look straight to the gospels and note the pattern and model shown by Jesus for making disciples. The first disciples were simply called to follow Him. No formal "altar call," no promises of a problem-free life. Just an invitation to journey along to witness His interactions with people, the demonstration of the Kingdom and to receive teachings about His Kingdom and how to live in it. They were given the values and principles that contrasted life in this world and life in the Kingdom.

Other disciples came along on their own volition, deciding to follow after witnessing the power and the truths. Some followed long term, many others fell away. Jesus made it clear that following Him would not be a picnic. It would be a costly choice as this world was no friend of His or any that would follow.

In making disciples there are a few notable actions exercised by Jesus. There was a challenge to repent or turn away from embracing lifeless, dead works, worthless things of this world and things not having eternal value. They were challenged to pick up their own painful cross and follow Him. It was made clear that choosing to follow Him meant they would have to completely adjust their priorities. It was Him and His Kingdom that they would be expected to pledge their allegiance to above all else. This included putting in proper perspective their material things, religious systems and even family. He taught them to pray and fast and how to interact with the Father. He taught them compassion, how to serve and how to love.

In discipleship, I like to look for a progressive transformation, something that comes from within, something deeper than Scripture memorization, church attendance or serving on a church ministry.

I'm looking for self-directed, self-governing obedience to the Word of God, not religious rule keeping. A hunger for righteousness, a desire to share one's faith either directly or by a compelling lifestyle. A good grasp of Biblical truths, a free-flowing functioning in the gifts of the Spirit and manifested fruit of the Spirit, not just behavior modification.

Jesus was willing to pour into anyone who was willing to submit to the process. If they rejected what He was offering, He had no issue with moving on. There has to be a mutual willingness.

I am motivated to live out this biblical pattern, even producing new hymns, phrases and narratives that articulate this Jesus way of making disciples.

"When we care for
ourselves as our very
own beloved—with naps,
healthy food, clean sheets,
a lovely cup of tea—we
can begin to give in wildly
generous ways to the
world, from abundance."

- Anne Lamott

LEADERS AND SELF-CARE

Without question, the Pandemic has taken its toll on all of us. No one has gone unscathed. Church leaders serving behind the digital pulpit have also been negatively impacted. From pivoting away from physical spaces to virtual, to quarantine isolation and suffering loss of friends and family. Some have also had to watch helplessly as colleagues succumbed to this vicious virus.

These stresses and pressures have all made it easy to turn away from self-care and neglect our own wellbeing. I would like to admonish every leader to give attention to yourselves. We are not exempt from stress, anxiety, depression or even fear. Our wholeness is primary as we endeavor to serve others.

Burnout

Mondays used to be my firm day off. As of this writing that is no longer the case, and in fact my day off is now a floating one, as I am still struggling to regain my equilibrium. So many demands are now out of sequence; mindfully setting out to become reoriented is going to be key to avoiding burnout. We have had so many things come at us so quickly that we have yet to fully calculate the changes needed since the onset of this Pandemic. It may now take some innovation and out-of-the-box thinking to create schedules that give us room to take regular breaks and feel refreshed on a consistent basis. The following provides more details on practical steps to take to prevent burnout that may result from this current crisis.

Zoom Fatigue

Spending too many hours in front of a computer screen hosting or attending various meetings can easily result in "Zoom fatigue." Zoom fatigue is a newly coined term used to describe the stress and exhaustion that comes from having to be "on" all the time during virtual meetings. Gloria Sherrod, a Licensed Professional Counselor says,

A majority of our communication in person is non-verbal. We often know what certain body language means without the other person having to verbalize it. With video calls, we miss out on a great deal of that because we are only seeing talking heads. Due to this fact, we sometimes may be working double time to process and convey information we are hearing on the other side of the call. Not to mention we are seeing ourselves all the time which can cause us to become self-conscious. We may not think of the exhaustion this can cause because of the convenience of just hosting a call, so we have to be conscious to not overdo it.

Practically speaking, don't feel compelled to attend every meeting. Just because you can, and they are easily accessible, doesn't mean you should. Try to avoid a lot of back-to-back meetings and gatherings and don't be afraid to say no and decline offers to join those that are non-essential. If you're responsible for scheduling virtual meetings, consider establishing policy that restricts meeting times to no more than an hour and, ideally, try to keep them within thirty-minute segments. Creating clear agendas can prevent meetings from getting unnecessarily long as well.

Mental health

As leaders, we shoulder an enormous amount of responsibility. Many of the stresses that we experience can go undetected; they can lie beneath the surface or not be understood. These manifest in different ways such as in mood swings, insomnia and feelings of sadness and even hopelessness. Many leaders can experience episodic anxiety and low-level depression. Having people with whom you can share your feelings is good, and of course we should not be reluctant to seek professional counseling as a viable option. Sherrod notes that we should "acknowledge the difficulty which may come from being in a helping position and feeling like you must "have it all together." Sherrod further suggests that, "accepting and acknowledging our own difficulties is what will help us to be able to continue to help others." When we choose to disregard our struggles or push them aside because we feel they "aren't allowed," they inevitably stay with us as the elephant in the room, until we choose to address them. Adding that experiencing anxiety or depression is no more a reflection of faithlessness than experiencing the common cold.

Emotional Health

We are emotional beings, not robots and it's important to be able to emote as needed. But to do so requires that we are emotionally healthy. No one should deny all of what they are feeling and experiencing inside, especially during these times. Remember Jesus wept, sighed and sometimes vented His anger.

I had to bury two members of my church during the Pandemic. It was painful to not be able to engage the families as in normal times, and it was painful to tell them I couldn't be present at certain intervals of the process. This is something many leaders have experienced, adding to their emotional drain.

Here are some things I've tried to practice to sustain good mental health:

- Physical exercise
- Reading a variety of materials
- Staying busy with unrelated productive things

- Cooking meals at home
- Connecting with friends who are comfortable with my humanity
- Watching my diet, and trying to eat foods that promote good mental health
- Prayer and meditation
- Listening to soothing music, especially in the morning and evenings before bed

Fear and anxiety

Not only are we dealing with the discomfort and inconvenience of not having access to our facilities as before, we are also dealing with the unknowns and the uncertainties about the future. These can produce fear and anxiety, causing us to nose dive into dark places. As we attempt to navigate these experiences, it can be difficult. What can often make it even more challenging for leaders, who are looked to as a source of strength and steadfastness. But we too are human, and when we are caught unaware, we can be negatively impacted. Accept the fact that you're not exempt. Healthy practices are essential, but I repeat: Reach out for help if you are feeling overwhelmed.

Rest and Boundaries

As we struggle to regain our equilibrium, setting boundaries is a must, otherwise we are likely to overdo it. Establish some good rest habits and sleep goals. I am finding short, late afternoon naps to be most beneficial. Invite your family and team to help you. Let them sound the alarm

when you are overextending yourself. This is vital to your mental, emotional and physical health.

Boundaries can be difficult for pastors in general, and especially when everyone is accessible with the click of a button. Remember that you can say no to a new commitment, you can decline a phone call, and you do not have to be responsible for absolutely everything. If you say yes to everything, you will be on E before you know it.

Spiritual Health

Maintaining spiritual health is easily and frequently neglected. This is especially true for leaders, as our lives are consumed with the work of ministry, and we can make ourselves believe that work is our intimacy. Well, it's not. Make sure to set aside time to pray and spend time in God's Word and presence. Reading good books for personal consumption and not for study is also good. Invite a friend or your spouse to check in to make sure you're maintaining your spiritual disciplines.

In a recent conversation with one of our young professionals, noticing his absence at church, I stressed the importance of balance, making sure every base was covered and tended to in appropriate measures. It's really easy to become hyper-focused on one aspect of life and allow others to be neglected. We need to allocate sufficient time and presence to self, family, work and spiritual intimacy.

Physical Health

Taking care of our physical health is vital. Both the personal day-to-day maintenance and having a relationship with a personal physician with whom you partner to keep you in optimum health.

It is vital that you start—or maintain—an exercise routine. With so much more time spent in front of the computer, we are quickly becoming akin to a sack of potatoes—lumpy and bumpy all over. If you have an established exercise routine, it is imperative that you continue. If you don't have one, then start with something as simple as walking for 15-20 minutes per day. If you prefer going to the gym, investing in a personal trainer is a good idea.

Exercise will strengthen your heart and improve your blood circulation. Increased blood flow raises the oxygen levels in your body, which helps lower your risk of heart diseases such as high cholesterol, coronary artery disease, and heart attack. Regular exercise can also lower your blood pressure and triglyceride levels.

With all of the aforementioned things, I can tell you that when the mental, emotional and spiritual are neglected, they will have a direct impact on your physical health. The approach to all of this should be a holistic and balanced one, while attending to the whole man, body, soul and spirit.

"A bend in the road is
not the end of the road...
Unless you fail to make the
turn."

- Helen Keller

IN SUMMATION

The COVID-19 global pandemic has forever changed the world, and impacted the Church in significant ways as well. As a church leader for over a quarter century, I was inspired to pen my thoughts to present some recent historical perspectives, site some observations, offer some suggestions on how we might navigate this period and, at the very least, prompt some thinking and dialogue concerning the entire experience. My hope is to contribute to the Church seizing the moment to move forward into this new era having become relevant, stronger and better equipped to meet the challenges ahead.

I think we would all agree that the Church has been experiencing a shift in the last decade or so, which has led us to rethink about how we do church and even why we do church. We've had to closely examine our methods, motives and practices, asking difficult questions of ourselves about our efficacy, particularly given the emerging global landscape that now exists. While technology has played a significant role in this shift, the response to the disruption has varied. Unfortunately, many have chosen to ignore it and not keep pace.

The Pandemic has accelerated this inevitable, drastic and compelling change. Without any advanced notice, churches all over the world have been forced to cease business as usual and find alternative ways to dispense the gospel, while maintaining healthy community.

Having no time to think or prepare, we had to quickly pivot. Some are prepared better than others, but no matter the ministry, the playing field has been leveled and most every ministry has had to shift from familiarity of our physical spaces, to the unknowns of the virtual pulpit.

In this writing, I've shared some of my own experiences with navigating this shift. I wanted to document some of these historic events, while also looking to connect with those traveling along this same road. While we've all managed in our own unique ways, certainly there are some commonalities and I thought to frame these to provide narrative for the unfolding journey.

Some of the questions I've tried to address include: What will the future hold for the Church? What has this shift produced? Will this mean the undoing of some things that needed to be undone? Will we see lasting change or will things just return to the way they've always been? Some call it a return to normalcy. But the question is, what is normal now? Many things have been disclosed, uncovering our strengths, weaknesses and the quality of our spiritual walk.

The truth is, ministry delivered virtually has proven to be effective in some very surprising ways. It has challenged us to consider the way church is executed on many levels; specifically, how we embrace and incorporate technology in a healthy way, while maintaining the integrity of biblical patterns.

There are reports of unprecedented spiritual growth in virtual spaces. Many churches are reporting sustained and even some increased financial support There's been an accountability shift, where people are taking greater responsibility for their own spiritual development. With less to judge, as in the case of physical spaces, with fewer distractions, attendees are more focused. The convenience has meant more regular attendance and with travel times eliminated, those who may have been unable to attend—due to work schedules, illness, etc.—are now participating more. Much of the energy previously expended is now being redirected and given to better spiritual self-care. There are many other benefits arising out of this transition as well.

It's a good time for the Church to reflect and reassess her impact and how this forced immersion might be leading us to a place of needed reformation. We have an opportunity to seize the moment and progress forward giving the Church new life, while greatly expanding our ministry footprint. No longer just a local work, even a storefront sized ministry can take their ministries global. I foresee new pioneers emerging who will lead us into this new era, introducing us to new models and helping us to take advantage of this Spirit-led momentum.

May the Spirit of God aid in our imagining, exploring and experimenting.

BIOGRAPHY

Nolan W. McCants is founder and Senior Pastor of Harvest Church Plainfield, a thriving ministry in south/west suburban Chicago. He has written and published a number of books, is an international speaker, businessman and award-winning fine arts photographer. He serves on the board of the International Communion of Charismatic Churches. As a practical teacher, he emphasizes the role of the church in the earth today. He is a frequent lecturer on the subject throughout the world.

Contact:
Nolan W. McCants
P. O. Box 9352
Naperville, IL 60567-9352
630.904.6262
www.thedigitalpulpit.org

Made in the USA
Middletown, DE
26 July 2021

44829128R00046